SHRED IT!

BANK IT
EXTREME BMX FREESTYLE

Virginia Loh-Hagan

45TH PARALLEL PRESS

Ann Arbor, Michigan

www.cherrylakepublishing.com

Content Adviser: Liv Williams, Editor, iLivExtreme

Reading Adviser: Beth Walker Gambro, MS, Ed., Reading Consultant, Yorkville, IL

Photo Credits: © georgeolsson/iStock.com, cover, title page; © homydesign/Shutterstock, 5; © A.RICARDO/Shutterstock, 6; © Konrad Swierad/Shutterstock, 7; © Haslam Photography/Shutterstock, 9; © conzorb/Shutterstock, 11; © homydesign/Shutterstock, 12; © Johanna Phillips Huuva/Shutterstock, 13; © Konrad Swierad/Shutterstock, 15; © smileimage9/Shutterstock, 16; © Dmitry Elagin/Shutterstock, 17; © Mihail Fedorenko/Shutterstock, 18–19; © Phillip Gray/Dreamstime.com, 20; © homydesign/Shutterstock, 21; © Vaughan Pickhaver/Shutterstock, 22; © Haslam Photography/Shutterstock, 25; © Haslam Photography/Shutterstock, 26; Nicholas Sheard, CC BY-SA 4.0 via Wikimedia Commons, 28; © WENN/Alamy, 29

Library of Congress Cataloging-in-Publication Data has been filed and is available at catalog.loc.gov

Cherry Lake Press would like to acknowledge the work of the Partnership for 21st Century Learning, a Network of Battelle for Kids. Please visit Battelle for Kids online for more information.

Printed in the United States of America

Note from publisher: Websites change regularly, and their future contents are outside of our control. Supervise children when conducting any recommended online searches for extended learning opportunities.

ABOUT THE AUTHOR

Virginia Loh-Hagan is an author, university professor, former classroom teacher, and curriculum designer. In college, she jumped off a bunk bed and broke her toe. No more jumping for her. She lives in San Diego with her very tall husband and very naughty dogs.

Table of Contents

About the Author 2

CHAPTER 1:
No Excuses! 4

CHAPTER 2:
Going Off Track 10

CHAPTER 3:
There's a Style for Every Rider! 14

CHAPTER 4:
Keep Shredding! 24

Did You Know? 30
Consider This! 31
Learn More 31
Glossary 32
Index 32

CHAPTER 1

No Excuses!

Extreme BMX bikers don't give up. They don't stop trying. They don't make excuses. They fall. But they get back up. Why? They want to be the best.

They speed up **half-pipes**. Half-pipes are U-shaped ramps. Bikers spin upside down. They try to **land**, or complete, tricks.

Extreme BMX bikers try to get the highest **air**. Getting air means soaring high in the air. Bikers ride up a giant **quarterpipe**. A quarterpipe is half of a U-shaped ramp. Some riders have reached more than 25 feet (7.6 meters) in the air!

Extreme BMX bikers don't let gravity stop them!

Extreme BMX riders like landing big new tricks. Some try riding BMX bikes down a **Mega Ramp**. This is a really huge ramp. It can be 62 to 74 feet (18.6 to 22.6 m) tall! Bikers jump across a big gap. They fly high into the air. They do tricks.

One trick is called a backflip barspin. Riders grab the handlebars. They spin them around. They do this in the middle of a backflip! Riders are always inventing new challenges.

SHRED IT! SPOTLIGHT:

Nikita Ducarroz

Nikita Ducarroz is a professional BMX freestyler. She struggles with anxiety and depression. It made it hard for her to leave the house as a young teenager. She thought that BMX looked like fun. She started practicing. She made friends with other BMX riders. She said they felt like family. Then, she started competing. All of this helped her deal with her anxiety. Ducarroz is a big mental health **advocate**. An advocate speaks up for people or things they believe in. Ducarroz works hard to support other action sports athletes.

NIKITA DUCARROZ

That's what BMX riding is all about. Riders push limits. Freestyling is about creativity and courage. Riders are always improving. They add their own twists to classic stunts. Riders spend hours practicing.

Kevin Robinson made no excuses. He was a BMX legend. He was the first to land a double flair. That's 2 backflips while spinning in the air. In 2017, he set a world record for highest air at 27 feet (8.2 m). He broke about 25 bones in his career. He had at least 50 blows to the head. He had 45 surgeries. Robinson died in 2017 of a stroke. But he is still remembered.

Kevin Robinson performs in Salt Lake City a month after winning gold at the 2009 X Games in Los Angeles.

CHAPTER 2

Going Off Track

BMX stands for bicycle **motocross**. Motocross is when riders race motorcycles around dirt tracks.

BMX riding started in the 1960s. It started in Southern California. It started as bike racing. Dirt tracks were tough on the riders' bikes. They would land hard on their bikes. Bikes bent. Wheels broke.

Tires were flattened. Riders needed better bikes. They changed bikes to fit their needs. They made them lower. This made bikes stronger.

BMX bikes turn quickly. They handle jumps easily. They have small wheels. The tires have **knobbies**, or bumps. The knobbies grip the dirt. BMX bikes have **pegs**. Pegs are rods on the side of the bike. Riders stand on the pegs to do tricks.

In the late 1970s, BMX riding changed. Bob Haro landed the first "rock walk" trick. BMX freestyle riding was born.

Riders started riding in skate parks. They rode in empty swimming pools. They stood on their bike seats. They popped **wheelies**. Wheelies are when the front wheel is off the ground.

EXTREME BMX FREESTYLE:

Know the Lingo

Bail: pulling out of a trick to avoid wiping out

Bank: use a sloped surface

Dabbing: putting a foot on the ground to help balance; also called foot down

Dialed: doing a trick correctly

Fakie: riding backward

Gnarly: beyond rad, beyond extreme, perfection; dangerous

Huck: throwing yourself into a trick

Nothing: taking both hands and feet off the bike

Potato chip: wheel that gets bent

Rad: cool, radical

Road rash: long, painful scrapes caused by wiping out

Roller: single jump on a hill

Shred: to ride fast and hard

Sidewalking: hopping sideways

Step up: one small jump followed by a larger one

Whip: throwing the bike to the side in midair

Whoop-de-dos: series of small hills; also called rollers

POTATO CHIP

CHAPTER 3

There's a Style for Every Rider!

Not all BMX freestyle riding is the same. There are different types. Some riders switch between different types. They choose what they think is more fun. They choose what challenges them.

Stunt riding is one type. There are fewer rules in stunt riding. The riders are free to create tricks. Other styles are different. They have strict rules. The rules can make tricks harder.

Falling is a big part of extreme BMX freestyle riding. Riders have many words for falling. They include: bail, slam, wipe out, eat it, and crash and burn. Helmets and pads keep riders safe.

FLATLAND RIDING

Flatland riders do tricks on smooth ground. Riders flip bikes into unusual positions. Riders spin and balance on one wheel. They can touch anything on their bikes. But they can't touch the ground. They can't stop riding until their routines are done.

Street riding is the most popular form of BMX freestyle. Street riders use city streets and **obstacles**. Obstacles are objects in the way. Riders do tricks on curbs, stairs, and benches. They **grind**, or slide. They jump. They often don't use brakes.

STREET RIDING

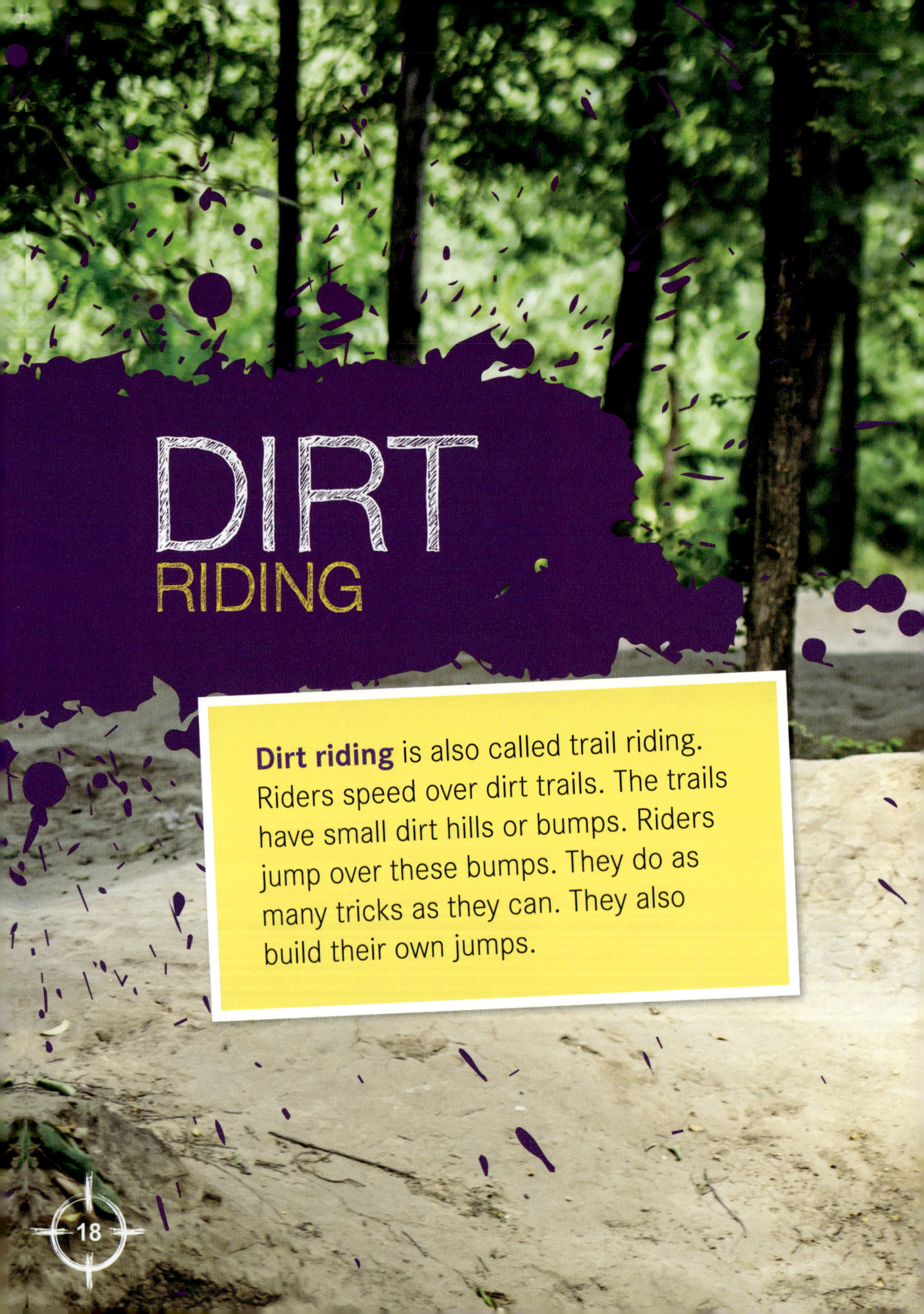

DIRT RIDING

Dirt riding is also called trail riding. Riders speed over dirt trails. The trails have small dirt hills or bumps. Riders jump over these bumps. They do as many tricks as they can. They also build their own jumps.

PARK RIDING

Park riders do tricks in skateboard parks. They ride up curved ramps. They jump over boxes. They do tricks in the air.

Vertical riders speed up big bike ramps and pipes. They launch into the air. They do tricks. Their goal is to get vertical. They want to get straight up into the air.

VERTICAL RIDING

SHRED IT! SPOTLIGHT:
Mat Hoffman

Mat Hoffman is a famous BMX vertical rider. Some say he is the best of all time. He set a world air record in 2001. That's the record Kevin Robinson broke. Hoffman taught Robinson. Hoffman does many daring stunts. He rode his bike off a cliff in Norway. The cliff is 3,200 feet (975 m) above ground. He did two backflips. Then he opened a parachute. He glided safely to the ground.

Hoffman won a gold medal with 3 broken bones in his foot. He is known as "The Condor." A condor is a large bird. Hoffman looks like he's flying. He's the first person to complete a no-handed 900. A 900 is $2\frac{1}{2}$ spins in the air.

MAT HOFFMAN

CHAPTER 4

Keep Shredding!

BMX riders show that success isn't easy.

Dave Mirra knew all about falling and getting up. He was hit by a drunk driver. He was crossing the street. It almost killed him. Doctors told him he couldn't ride again. Mirra didn't let that stop him.

Dave Mirra died tragically in 2016. In 2024, his family and others founded The Dave Mirra Foundation. It celebrates and honors his legacy. It promotes safe cycling, mental health awareness, and youth sports and wellbeing programs.

It took him 6 months to heal. He got back on his bike. He won several gold medals. He said, "It was a setback, but something I overcame. It doesn't even mess with me at all."

Mirra invented his own stunts. His nickname is "Miracle Man." He did a double backflip. This is a hard trick. Both rider and bike do 2 backflips in the air.

He said, "Anything you want to get better at is a commitment. Without commitment, there would be no success."

Hannah Roberts is another committed BMX freestyle rider. She won gold at the Urban World Championships 6 times! She won gold at the Pan American Games.

Hannah Roberts performs a trick in the UCI Urban World Championships.

Roberts rode in the 2020 Tokyo Olympics. But her foot slipped on her pedal. She broke her foot. She still took home a silver medal. Her foot healed. She kept riding.

Extreme BMX riders don't let anything get in their way.

SHRED IT!
VOICE FROM THE FIELD:

Aaron Fotheringham

Aaron Fotheringham definitely makes no excuses. He was born with a health condition. He cannot use his legs. But that didn't stop him from being a BMX rider. Fotheringham went with his brother to a skateboard park. His brother told him to try riding on the ramp on his wheelchair. Fotheringham did. He fell on his face. But he didn't quit. He kept practicing. He learned to do crazy tricks on his wheelchair. He uses moves from BMX free riding and skateboarding. He said, "I'm so pumped to be able to get out there and show people what a wheelchair can do. That it doesn't hold you back." He has a special wheelchair. It is built for stunts. He set a world record. He did the first complete backflip in a wheelchair.

AARON FOTHERINGHAM

DID YOU KNOW?

- Women are crushing it in BMX. Linda Grabner is a street rider who does lots of cool stunts. Macarena Pérez Grasset is a BMX park rider. She also likes BMX trail riding. She travels around the world to compete.

- Matthias Dandois is a BMX world champion. Sam Partaix is a professional BMX rider. They jumped on their bikes into a water-filled swimming pool. They were at a private castle in France. They did BMX tricks underwater.

- BMX tricks are given names. Tricks are usually named by their inventors. For example, Bill Nitschke landed a trick in a Burger King parking lot. He named the trick "Whopper." It is also known as a "bunnyhop tailwhip."

- Extreme BMX freestyle riders have their own language. Try to understand this: "He got a nothing to rail done. He also nothing'd down the stairs and did a nose wheelie to footjam over the volcano."